Hayner Public Library District-Alton
0 00 30 0217986 3

P9-CQH-239

DATE DUE			

INSECT
WARS

INSECT WARS

SARA VAN DYCK

A FIRST BOOK

FRANKLIN WATTS
A Division of Grolier Publishing
New York • London • Hong Kong • Sydney
Danbury, Connecticut

ACKNOWLEDGMENTS

My thanks to the many people who have contributed so generously with expertise, suggestions, and support. Special thanks go to John Rodgers of Buena Biosystems in Santa Paula, California; Patricia Gordon and the staff of the Santa Monica Public Library in California; and especially the staff of the Children's Department.

Photographs ©: Bill Beatty: 13; Buena Biosystems, Ventura, CA: cover, 15, 42, 43; Disney Enterprises, Inc.: 47; Jeffrey D. Hahn: 16, 51; Photo Researchers: 8 (Dr. Jeremy Burgess/SPL), 2 (Stephen Dalton), 17, 52 (Holt Studios International), 23 (J. H. Robinson), 22, 54 (Harry Rogers), 20 (Jerome Wexler); Superstock, Inc.: 11, 35; Valan Photos: 37 (Y. R. Tymstra); Visuals Unlimited: 25, 45 (J. Alcock), 27 (Bill Beatty), 39 (John D. Cunningham), 31 (Robert Lindholm), 29 (Science VU).

Library of Congress Cataloging-in-Publication Data
van Dyck, Sara
Insect wars / Sara van Dyck.
p. cm. (A First book)
Includes bibliographical references and index.
Summary: Discusses several types of beneficial insects and how they are being raised by insectaries and purchased by farmers, theme park operators, and restaurant owners to protect food crops and decorative vegetation.
ISBN 0-531-20261-5 (lib. bdg.) ISBN 0-531-15857-8 (pbk.)
1. Insect pests—Biological control—Juvenile literature. 2. Agricultural pests—Biological control—Juvenile literature. 3. Insects as biological pest control agents— Juvenile literature. [1. Insect pests—Control. 2. Agricultural pests—Control. 3. Insects as biological pest control agents.] I. Title. II. Series.
SB933.3.V37 1997
632'.7—dc20 96-25874
CIP
AC

Printed in the United States of America.
1 2 3 4 5 6 7 8 9 10 R 05 04 03 02 01 00 99 98 97

CONTENTS

INTRODUCTION

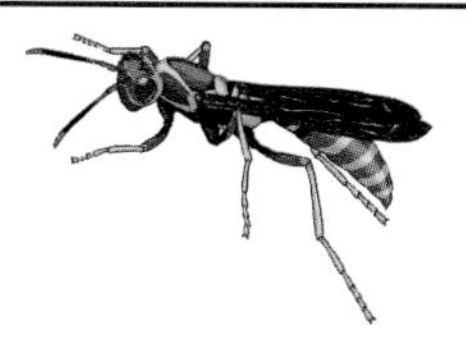

Aphids in a local park are attacking the roses. Caterpillars in a vegetable garden are munching on the ear of corn you hoped to eat for dinner. Elm trees, petunias, lettuce, strawberries—insects are out to get them all.

Not all insects destroy the plants humans eat. Many beetles and flies help break down and recycle dead animals, garbage, or rotting wood. In addition, many insects are an important source of food for other animals. Fish eat mayflies. Many of our favorite songbirds include a variety of insects in their diets. Many plants could not live without the bees and moths that transfer *pollen* from one flower to another.

Aphids pierce plant tissues and suck out the sap.
They live in colonies of fifty or more and can produce
more than ten generations in one season.

It's hard to imagine a world without insects. They are everywhere. In fact, more than three-quarters of the *species* named and described by scientists are insects. Luckily for us, there are as many helpful insects as there are destructive ones. These helpful insects, called *beneficials*, are constantly battling the ones that feed on plants. Without beneficials, our gardens, crop fields, orchards, and parks would be stripped bare by pests.

Scientists who study insects are called *entomologists*. Some entomologists explore remote parts of the globe, hunting for new types of insects. Others work in laboratories, raising insects and learning about their life cycles. Still others tramp through fields, sweeping large collecting nets to gather insects and advising farmers how to combat pests.

Many entomolgists first become interested in insects when they are young. They all start by learning the names of insects—including beneficials—that they see every day. You're probably already familiar with some beneficials, such as ladybugs. Other helpful insects, like certain *larvae* or parasitic wasps, aren't so well known.

Once you know what to look for, however, you will be able to spot them easily. If you learn what pests particular beneficials attack, how they behave, and where they live, you can locate a variety of helpful insects. As you watch them, you will see for yourself what happens when insects go to war.

CHAPTER 1

THE HUNTERS

There are two types of beneficials: predators and parasites. Insect *predators*, such as ladybugs, green lacewings, and hover flies, are meat-eaters. They hunt and eat other insects, just as wolves eat other *mammals* and sharks eat other fish.

LADYBUGS

The best-known predatory insect is the ladybug. Of the roughly 400 different species of ladybugs found in North America, all but two are beneficial.

Ladybugs are especially attracted to *aphids*, one of the most serious and common garden pests. Aphids are tiny

It may take a ladybug more than 5 minutes to polish off an aphid—but not even a scrap of its prey will remain.

insects that attack plants growing on farms, in small towns, and even in large cities. These insects are often green and usually form clusters on apple trees, tomatoes, rose bushes, American elms, and many other plants. They cling to the leaves, stems, or flowers of plants and suck out the juices. Eventually, the plant droops, the leaves shrivel, and the flowers drop.

Ladybugs are actually beetles, not bugs. One of the differences between bugs and beetles is that beetles have chewing mouthparts while bugs' mouthparts are adapted for sucking. Ladybugs chew up aphids with their razor-sharp *mandibles*, or jaws.

In warm spring weather, look for ladybugs hunting in colonies of aphids. They crawl over the aphids, pluck them off the plant, and slowly crunch each aphid body—bit by bit.

Ladybugs have enormous appetites. A ladybug can eat about fifty aphids a day. Ladybugs aren't fussy eaters. Besides aphids, they also devour tiny worms, caterpillars, mites, scale insects, whiteflies, or whatever else they can get their little mouthparts on.

Ladybug *larvae* are also predators. Since larvae are growing, they are even more hungry than adult ladybugs. One larva may gobble up more than 300 aphids during the week or two it takes to grow into an adult.

The larva looks similar to a stubby lizard and scurries about actively on its six legs. Its colors are the reverse of a

A ladybug larva eats the larva of the
asparagus beetle and other harmful insects.

ladybug's—a ladybug has black spots on red wings, while the larva has red or blue spots on a black body. When it finds an aphid, the larva pierces its prey with its hollow mandibles and sucks out the juices.

You also might spot ladybug eggs on the underside of a leaf. To the naked eye they look like small yellow grains, but with a hand magnifier, you can see the clumps of tiny golden eggs.

GREEN LACEWINGS

The green lacewing is not as famous as the ladybug, but it is just as effective. Adults are nocturnal (active at night). You can often find them flying around window screens on a summer night. They eat aphids, pollen, and *honeydew* (a sticky, sweet material excreted by insects like aphids and scales).

Green lacewing larvae are one of the top pest destroyers. During the day, they crawl about on leaves searching for aphids, red spider mites, mealybugs, eggs of many worms, and other harmful insects. When they find prey, they pierce it with their curved front pincers and drain out the body fluids. Their appetite is so great that they are often called "aphid lions." One larva can eat up to sixty aphids in an hour.

Green lacewing larvae have the same shape as ladybug larvae, but they are often tan or black. Although the larvae are common, they are so small and dull in color that they are difficult to locate.

This lacewing larva is draining the body fluids from an aphid. Although lacewing larvae are only about twice as big as aphids, they can kill hundreds of these pests during their 2-week larval stage.

HOVER FLIES

You've almost certainly seen hover flies. They are one of the most valuable beneficials because they protect many kinds of flowers. Their black, orange, and yellow bands make them look

A hover fly, which resembles a bee, can hover—or hang almost still—in midair.

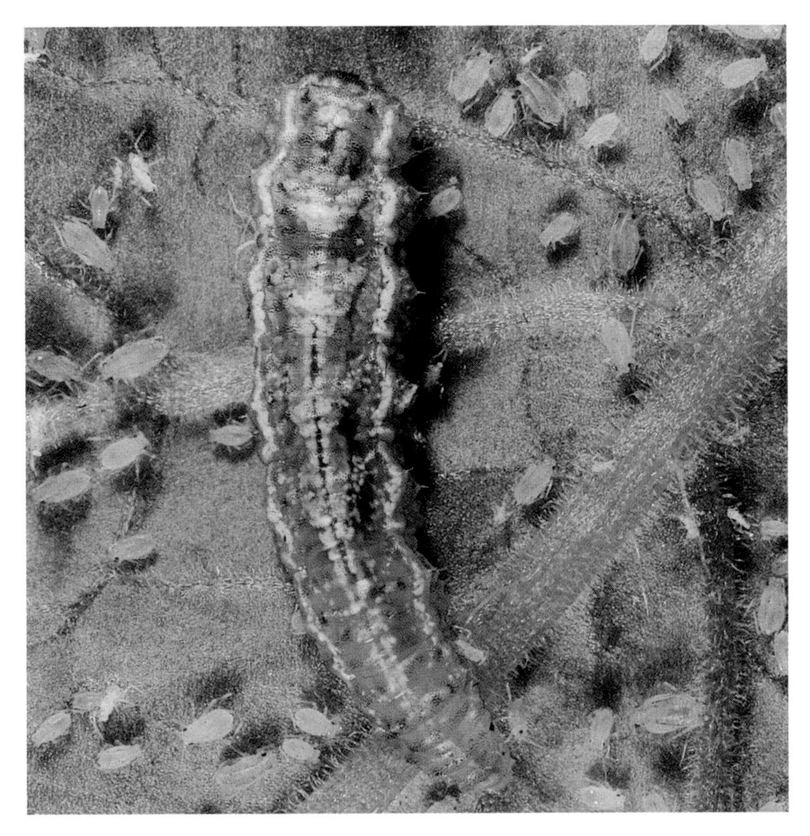

The hover fly larva grabs one aphid after another, hoists it up, and sucks out its body juices.

like small, slim bees. Unlike bees, hover flies can remain almost completely stationary above a flower. Hover flies have only two wings, while bees have four. Adult hover flies feed on nectar, but the larvae are great predators of aphids and mealybugs.

Hover fly larvae are easy to observe as they feed on aphids clustered on a rosebush or wildflower. Look for a small, pale-green caterpillar with a white stripe down its back. Each larva is about three-quarters of an inch (2 cm) long.

The larvae crawl slowly among aphids clustered on the tops of leaves or in the area where leaves meet the stem. Each larva noses about until it finds its prey, which it grasps with its mouth hooks and lifts over its head. It then sucks the body fluids from the aphid until only its *exoskeleton* (skinlike outer layer) is left. The larva drops the empty bits and goes on to its next victim.

You don't need a magnifier to watch a larva feeding, but if you do have one, you can watch the aphid changing color and shrinking as its fluids are extracted. To get the best view, take a small square of firm, white paper or an index card and carefully scoop up one of the larvae. Then shake or scrape a few of the aphids off a leaf, place them in front of the larva, and watch it chow down. Be sure to carefully place the larva back on the leaf where you found it, so that it can continue its good work!

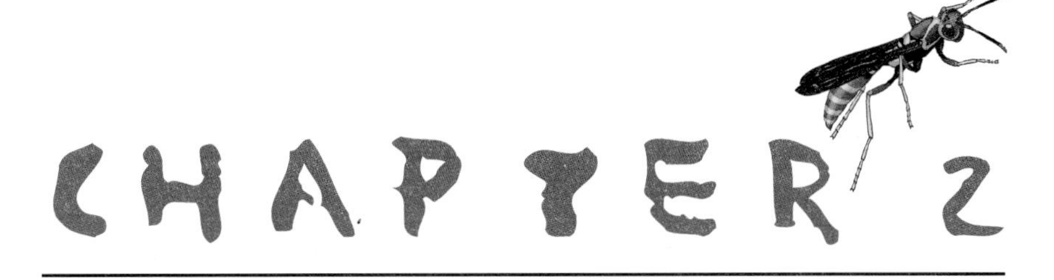

IT'S AN INSIDE JOB

While predators boldly stalk their prey, parasitic beneficials use a sneaky approach to attack destructive insects.

PARASITIC WASPS

Like their relatives, the wasps and bees you're familiar with, parasitic wasps dart about on two pairs of wings. Some feed on sweets, but they also have a grisly mission.

A female parasitic wasp lays her eggs on or inside the body of a caterpillar. Insects that place their eggs inside the host are called *endoparasites*. (The prefix "endo-" means "within.") When the larvae hatch, they feed on their victim's

This tiny parasitic wasp (with yellow spots) lays
its eggs inside gypsy moth larvae. The wasp's young
will hatch inside the host and feed on its body.

body. Since the caterpillar provides the food, it is called the *host.*

At first the larvae eat only the caterpillar's body fat, but as they grow, they eat more and more of the caterpillar's insides. By the time the larvae are fully grown, there is sometimes nothing left of the caterpillar but a bit of exoskeleton. Scientists call these wasps *parasitoids* because they always kill their host.

Although you can't watch a wasp larva chewing its prey as a predator does, you can sometimes notice the damage the wasp has done. For instance, you might notice a caterpillar with little white beads on its back. These are not eggs; they are the cocoons of wasp larvae. When the larvae are fully grown, they tunnel through the caterpillar's exoskeleton and spin their cocoons on top of the caterpillar.

Each spring, parasitic wasps search for hosts on garden plants, fruit trees, and shade trees. Farmers and gardeners welcome these wasps because the caterpillars that they invade are often the pests that destroy crops and leaves.

Almost every vegetable garden is visited by white cabbage butterflies, which have three black spots on their wings. The caterpillars they grow from munch holes in cabbage plants and other leafy vegetables. Parasitic wasps attack these caterpillars as well as greedy green tomato hornworms and corn earworms.

If you look closely at a female *ichneumon* wasp, you will see what looks like a long stinger at its tail end. This "stinger"

This tomato hornworm isn't carrying eggs on its back!
The white cases are the pupae, or cocoons, of a parasitic wasp.

is actually a thin tube used to deposit eggs. It is called an *ovipositor*. The female pushes the end of her ovipositor into the body of a host, such as a caterpillar, and releases her eggs.

Although there are more than 6,000 species of ichneumons, one kind is particularly common around homes. Look for a thin, orange and brown wasp with long antennae.

The female ichneumon wasp uses her long ovipositor, like a bent needle, to drill into the wood of a tree and reach a larva inside. She will lay her eggs near the larva so her young can eat it when they hatch.

It may be as much as 1 inch (2.5 cm) long. Although its sting is not very painful, you should avoid handling it and any other wasp.

Another kind of parasitic wasp you might see in action attacks aphids. These tiny wasps land on an aphid and jab their tail end into it. This tail end contains the ovipositor, which deposits the wasp eggs into the aphid.

Parasitic wasps come in a variety of sizes. One wasp, called Trichogramma, is only about the size of a pencil dot, but it kills more than 150 kinds of pests.

THE TACHINID FLY

Flies spread germs and diseases, so when you spot a fly you usually run for the swatter. But if you see what looks like a round-bottomed housefly crawling through leaves near the ground, take a closer look. This may be a tachinid fly, one of our best allies in controlling insect pests. The most common type of tachinid fly looks like it is covered with bristles and often has red or orange on the tip of its abdomen.

Like a bee, the tachinid fly sips nectar. As it travels from flower to flower, its hairs pick up pollen from one plant and carry it to another. Tachinid flies are also *parasites* that help control the population of cutworms and gypsy moth larvae.

You've probably seen parasitic wasps and tachinid flies without knowing what they were. In fact, almost any wasp or

Although it's related to the housefly that spreads disease, the colorful tachinid fly is a beneficial insect. Its larvae kill gypsy moth caterpillars and European corn borers.

fly you see flying around plants is beneficial. Without them we would enjoy few cherries or peaches, our vegetables would be full of holes, and our wheat fields would be devastated.

CHAPTER 3

YOU CAN'T ALWAYS TELL WHO THE GOOD GUYS ARE

There's one sure way to attract insects: have a picnic. You can count on some uninvited guests, the kind that crawl or fly. But before you start stomping and swatting, think about this: Ants, bees, and other annoying insects can actually be beneficial. In other words, some insects may be helpful at times and destructive at others. You can't always tell who the good guys are.

ANTS

The biggest problem with some ants—besides their interest in your picnic—is that they like sweets. Honeydew, the liquid produced by aphids and scale insects, is one of their favorite

These ants collect and eat the sweet honeydew excreted by aphids. In return for this meal, the ants offer the aphids protection from ladybugs and other enemies.

foods. Because they want honeydew, ants actually protect aphids. In fact, aphid colonies that are protected by ants reproduce more rapidly so they can turn out more honeydew.

If you find a branch loaded with aphids, chances are you'll also find ants. They will be crawling about among the aphids. If you touch the aphids, your fingers will become sticky with honeydew. When ladybugs or hover fly larvae attack the aphids, the ants may attack these predators because they are interfering with the ants' food source.

Although these ants make it easier for aphids to destroy plants, other types of ants are beneficial. Some ants eat the eggs and larvae of troublesome pests, such as the Mediterranean fruit fly. In Europe, one type of ant protects forests from destructive beetles. Hundreds of years ago, Chinese farmers placed ants near their orange trees so that they would devour harmful caterpillars.

To find out what foods ants prefer, try setting up an ant cafeteria. Place crumbs of various foods such as cookies, meat, cheese, and bread along an active ant trail and see what happens. (This works best if the food bits are very tiny—smaller than an ant.) Which food attracts the most ants? What do they do with the foods they choose?

WASPS AND PRAYING MANTIDS

Although wasps have a bad reputation and no one wants them at a picnic, larger wasps (the ones that are not parasitic) are often predators. Adult wasps catch other insects to feed their young. Their prey includes caterpillars, tomato hornworms, gypsy moths, and grasshoppers. Even nasty-tempered yellow jackets devour large numbers of pest insects.

Although many adult wasps eat honey or fruit juices, they also kill small insects such as aphids and take them home for their larvae to feed on.

Praying mantids are helpful because they eat aphids and caterpillars. However, they also prey on bees, parasitic wasps, and other beneficials. If you have a praying mantid in your garden, enjoy watching it, but don't count on it for much help.

SPIDERS

Because spiders have eight legs, rather than six, they are not insects. Spiders are, however, close relatives of insects. Both insects and spiders are *arthropods*, or animals with jointed legs.

When you see a spider, make it welcome. Spiders are beneficial because they eat many kinds of insects, helping to keep the general population of insects down. Some of the pests they eat are gypsy moths, crickets, destructive flies, and cockroaches.

BUTTERFLIES AND MOTHS

At your picnic, you may see colorful butterflies and moths. Although they are lovely, butterflies and moths hatch from larvae. In some cases, the larvae can be very destructive. As you learned in Chapter 2, the white cabbage butterfly is bad news. It develops from a caterpillar that dines on cabbages and other vegetables. The dark, dramatic-looking Sphinx

Spiders—including this crab spider—are some of nature's best pest controllers.

moth comes from the green tomato hornworm, one of the most damaging pests. Other larvae eat the leaves of shade trees or tunnel through apples.

Still, most butterflies and moths—including the famous Monarch butterfly—feed on wild plants and don't harm crops. As they visit plants to feed on nectar, they also pollinate the plants.

CHAPTER 4

THE PEST SOLUTION

Destroying harmful insects is a job farmers and gardeners have struggled with for centuries. In biblical times, people dreaded the hordes of locusts that swarmed in and devoured entire fields. Today, insects still do heavy damage to oranges, melons, lettuce, cotton, and many other crops. Hundreds of millions of dollars' worth of crops are destroyed by pests every year.

About 50 years ago, scientists thought that they had found the solution to this problem. They developed agricultural chemicals that were deadly to insects. These *pesticides*, such as DDT, could quickly wipe out entire populations of insects. By the 1960s, however, scientists discovered that these chemicals poisoned fish, birds, the workers that handled these chemicals, and the water supply. The pesticides also killed off the beneficial insects, and later the pests often came back in even greater numbers.

CONTROLLING INSECTS WITH INSECTS

In 1886, destructive scale insects attacked the orange groves of southern California. Within a few years, trees had withered and oranges stopped growing. Even though farmers sprayed their trees with chemicals, the scale insects continued to destroy trees. Desperate farmers burned their orchards and watched helplessly as all their work was lost.

Then a couple of scientists had a brilliant idea: why not use a beneficial insect to fight pests. They knew that there was a type of ladybug that eats scale insects in Australia. The scientists decided to bring this ladybug, called the Vedalia beetle, to California.

They released a box of only twenty-eight Vedalia beetles under an infested orange tree and the beetles went to war against the scale insects. As one local man put it, a "miracle" occurred. Soon, more Vedalias were imported and within 2 years the scale insect population was under control. To this day the Vedalia beetle continues to protect California's oranges.

Sometimes a sack of ladybugs released around trees or fields can do a better job controlling pests than *insecticides*.

This true story illustrates one of the most famous and successful examples of biological control, which is often called *biocontrol* for short. Biocontrol involves using beneficial insects to control harmful ones.

The goal of biocontrol is not to eliminate pest populations completely; it is to prevent them from doing too much damage to crops and other plants. Even if humans dislike aphids, tomato hornworms, and other pests, they are still an essential part of the chain of life. Some pests may have beneficial roles that we do not understand yet. Besides, we can live with a few holes on our vegetables or brown spots on our flowers.

BRING IN THE BUGS

So some entomologists—scientists who study insects—began to look for nonchemical ways to control pests. Many times, they found that the best way to get rid of a destructive insect is to bring in one that attacks it.

For example, the caterpillar of the white cabbage butterfly is a constant threat. In 1875, scientists found and imported a wasp that attacks this caterpillar. The wasp made itself at home and now darts around almost every cabbage patch across the country.

Since then, entomologists have brought in many other parasites. They've helped in controlling gypsy moths, satin moths (devourers of the leaves of shade trees), and the white-

The white cabbage butterfly may deposit as many
as several hundred yellow eggs on the underside of a leaf.
When the larvae emerge, they munch holes in
cabbage, broccoli, and brussels sprouts.

fly (which infests greenhouse plants). Another success story is the tachinid fly, which rescued Hawaiian sugarcane from the sugarcane borer.

Whenever a new pest threatens crops, agricultural scientists hunt for a beneficial to knock it out. Farmers have learned their lesson. They know that chemical pesticides are not the answer to their pest problems. It is likely that the field of biological control will continue to grow as more and more farmers search for safe ways to control pests.

BIODIVERSITY

So is biological control always the answer? Not necessarily. To make it work, the crops must grow near plants that attract the beneficials.

The food of choice for green lacewing adults is nectar, while larvae prefer aphids. As a result, lacewings will be attracted to sites that offer both food sources. If a gardener or farmer wants to protect a crop of lettuce from aphids, he or she should put flowering plants nearby.

Farmers and gardeners have learned that *biodiversity* (growing many different types of plants together) is important. Pest populations grow very quickly when they have access to a large area of land that contains only one type of crop plant. This is why the Colorado potato beetle became such a threat.

This Colorado potato beetle can destroy fields of potatoes, egg-plants, or peppers. Its range has spread across the United States and into France, Germany, and Italy.

Before the areas around the Rocky Mountains were settled, this beetle fed on the buffalo bur. These plants were scattered here and there, among a variety of other plants. Because the beetle had a number of natural predators, the number of potato beetles never increased too much.

When pioneers settled in this area, they cleared land and planted entire fields with nothing but potatoes. This was like giving the beetles a birthday party with all the cake and ice cream they could eat. They ate and ate and reproduced and reproduced until they had munched their way across the whole country. Because their predators did not reproduce as quickly, the balance of nature was upset. Today the Colorado potato beetle is still a serious pest in many states.

Many farmers still plant acre after acre of a single crop. This is how cotton, wheat, and corn are usually grown. Every once in a while, pest populations increase and destroy large quantities of these crops. Insects that were once only a minor nuisance have become a major problem.

Biocontrol is a word that scientists have made up to describe using one insect to control another. Even though the word is fairly new, the idea is very old. It has been occurring in nature for millions of years. Nature tends to keep things in balance. If the pest population grows too large, the number of beneficials will increase. Similarly, when the number of pests decreases, the number of beneficials will also decrease.

But sometimes there aren't enough beneficials to take care of the problem. If you're short on ladybugs, there is a solution—you can always buy some.

CHAPTER 5

INSECTS FOR SALE

Insects for sale? It sounds strange, doesn't it? But some beneficials are so useful that they are sold by mail order. You can actually buy a quart of ladybugs, a cup of lacewing eggs, or a card covered with wasp eggs. The beneficials that are shipped out go to work in orchards, greenhouses, nurseries, or on farms. In fact, many garden supply stores sell lacewing eggs to home gardeners.

Insects sold to farmers and researchers are raised in *insectaries*. The United States has ninety-five private insectaries or suppliers of beneficial insects, and Mexico and Canada have many more. One of these insectaries, Buena Biosystems, is located among the hills of southern California.

This cup contains 100,000 lacewing eggs. By the time the customer receives them, they will have developed into hungry larvae.

Insects are very fussy about how they grow, so the scientists at Buena Biosystems raise each type of insect in a separate room. Green lacewings, one of the most demanded beneficials, prefer warm rooms. Green lacewing eggs resemble green grains of sand. A worker places each egg in a cardboard cell. When the egg hatches, the larva stays in the cell and is

An insectary houses lacewing pupae in these containers, where they will grow into adult lacewings ready to lay more eggs.

fed until it develops into a *pupa*. The worker puts each pupa into a white cardboard tube the size of an oatmeal container. About 500 pupae fit into just one of these tubes. Rows of these containers line the shelves of another warm room.

Soon the pupae develop into adult lacewings, mate, and lay eggs of their own. Female lacewings lay each of their eggs on a threadlike stalk that projects from the side of the tube. After all the females have laid their eggs, the inside of the tube looks as though it's covered with a light green fuzz.

Now the lacewing eggs are ready to harvest. To do this, a worker collects the eggs by sweeping a cloth inside the tube and then shaking them into a large glass jar covered with a wire mesh.

Next, the worker spreads a thin mixture of glue and water on a card, holds the jar with the eggs upside down over the card, and shakes the jar—like a salt shaker—so that the eggs are sprinkled onto the card. The lacewing eggs are ready to sell. The insectary keeps some of the eggs, so that a new crop of lacewings can be grown and the cycle will continue.

Ladybugs, another big seller, are handled quite differently. Since they *hibernate* in large clusters during the winter, the easiest and least expensive way to obtain them is to collect them as they hibernate.

Workers hike through the mountains from late winter to the summer in search of ladybug clusters. Since the ladybugs are hibernating, they don't fly away. When workers find a cluster, they scoop up hundreds at a time, put them into

Ladybugs cluster for warmth when they hibernate.

burlap bags, load the bags into trucks, and drive them down to the insectary.

The sacks of ladybugs are placed in a cold shed that is kept at about the same temperature as your refrigerator, so that they will continue to hibernate. If a worker opens one of the sacks and places a few ladybugs on his or her palm, they will warm up and start to crawl around after a few minutes.

Insectaries also raise parasitic wasps. Trichogramma wasps are kept in warm cages. They insert their ovipositors and release their eggs into moth eggs that have been glued onto a strip of cardboard. The insectary then sells the cardboard strips with the wasp eggs safely inside the moth eggs. When the wasps hatch, they're ready to attack the pests.

BENEFICIALS AT THE MALL

Gardeners and farmers aren't the only ones that buy beneficials. Places the public visits, such as the Smithsonian Institution, the Missouri Botanical Garden, and many other botanic gardens and public parks, count on them to help protect their valuable plants. Walt Disney World in Florida uses them in their gardens and in the land pavilion at Epcot. By using beneficials, these places can control pests without using pesticides.

Indoor malls or outdoor restaurants sometimes buy parasitic wasps to protect their plants. Since they are very small

Beneficial insects are used to control pests at the land pavilion greenhouses at Epcot, part of Walt Disney World in Florida.

and they don't sting people, they can do their job without people even noticing them.

You may be wondering why people have to go out and buy insects. Don't insects just come on their own? After all, most of us see more ants, flies, and spiders than we want to.

Sometimes large numbers of beneficials are needed to curb pest populations that have grown so quickly that their natural predators just can't keep up with the problem. Buying beneficials may also be a good option for farmers who want to decrease the pest population without using chemical sprays.

CHAPTER 6

STOP, STOOP, AND SEARCH

Watching the beneficials at work isn't that tricky. You should be able to find them in just about any outdoor setting where no one is using chemical sprays—in a garden, a city park, or even a patch of weeds. (Sprays kill off pest insects, but they kill the beneficials, too.) Find a place where overeager gardeners don't get rid of all the larvae and cocoons as soon as they find them. If you look carefully, you can see tiny insects searching for prey or attacking other insects right in your own neighborhood.

The first thing you should do is stop, stoop, and search. Stop in front of a rose bush, a head of cabbage, or some chewed-up weed. Most beneficials are small, so you'll have to stoop down to get up close. Next, just look around.

First, check for flies or wasps flying around or sitting on the flowers. If there are no bees, see if you can spot any hover flies, ichneumons, or tachinid flies. Other tiny flying insects, too small to identify, might include gnats or parasitic wasps looking for a place to lay their eggs.

Now look at the growing tips of the leaves and examine the stems. If you can find some aphids—those tiny green or brown sucking bugs—you're in luck. If you do find a good crop of aphids, chances are that ladybugs, lacewings, hover flies, or their larvae are around too. If you don't see them, be patient. They are probably on their way. Look on the aphid colonies, the nearby leaves, and turn the leaves over to hunt for predators.

You use your eyes to search for insects, but how do ladybugs and other beneficials find their prey? First, they look for a particular *habitat*, or environment, and the kind of plant that usually has their prey on it. Then they rely on a combination of sight and smell to find individual pests. Ladybugs, for instance, may be able to smell the honeydew given off by aphids.

Finally, if you're looking in your own home garden or among weeds, gently separate the leaves and flower petals and look deep inside the flower. (Watch out for bees!) If you've seen butterflies or moths, be on the lookout for caterpillars. Some of these caterpillars may be covered with beady white cocoons left by parasitic wasps.

Find a colony of aphids—and the beneficials can't be far behind.

This green lacewing may be feeding on pollen, or looking for a place to lay its eggs.

When you do spot an insect, watch its behavior and ask yourself, "What's going on here?" Is the insect sipping nectar or searching for a mate? Is it chewing on a leaf or ready to suck the plant's vital sap? Is it hunting for a pest to eat or looking for a place to lay its eggs?

After you've observed insects for a while, you'll become familiar with the behavior of beneficials. Each insect has a favorite season, a favorite plant, a favorite prey.

KEEP HUNTING

On a day when you don't find any pests or beneficials, check for clues that pests have been present: leaves that are rolled or nibbled, cocoons, insect trails, or damaged fruit and flowers. If you see pests, but there are no beneficials around, be patient! Beneficials may arrive soon. It takes time for them to catch up with pests.

When you find plants that attract beneficials, keep going back to that location. The hover fly that you see one day may lay its eggs the next day, and soon you'll find the larvae feeding. In warm weather the entire life cycle of some insects, from egg to adult, takes as little as 1 month to complete. As you keep looking, you will get to know each stage of insect life.

The best times to look for beneficials are warm days in the spring and summer when plants are sprouting new

This giant ichneumon is attracted by a marigold. Flowering plants like Queen Anne's lace, fennel, and sweet alyssum offer beneficials nectar and pollen.

leaves. Pests like fresh growth because it's more tender and easier to feed on.

It's also exciting to search for beneficials at night. Look on windows or screens for lacewings or ichneumons that are attracted to the light. You can also poke into some bushes with a flashlight and broomstick. You never know what might come fluttering out!

BRINGING THEM HOME

If you want to attract beneficials to your garden, plant annuals such as marigolds, members of the sunflower family, or carrots. These plants are good sources of the nectar and pollen that many insects eat.

EQUIPMENT

All you really need to watch beneficials is a good pair of eyes, but a little equipment can make it more fun.

A small, hand magnifying glass can help you see the insects in greater detail. You can buy one at almost any local drugstore. To identify them, use an insect field guide. Be sure to choose one with as many photographs as possible.

You may also want to carry along a small, clear plastic cup or glass jar and an index card or piece of cardboard. When you find an interesting insect on a leaf, you can put the cup over it and slide the card underneath to keep the insect from flying away while you watch it.

After you've finished observing, be sure to place the bug back where you found it. After all, that creepy-looking creature may be one of our best friends!

GLOSSARY

aphid—a tiny sucking insect that feeds on plants such as roses.

arthropod—an animal such as an insect or spider that has legs with joints and an exoskeleton.

beneficial—good, helpful. Beneficial insects attack pests that damage crops or other plants.

biocontrol/biological control—using the natural enemies of a pest to keep its population down.

biodiversity—a variety of plant and animal life. The term is usually used to describe a particular habitat.

endoparasite—a parasite that lives inside its host.

entomologist—a biologist who studies insects.

exoskeleton—the outer, skinlike layer of all arthropods

habitat—the type of place where a plant or animal naturally lives. The woods, a flower garden, or a field are all kinds of habitat.

hibernate—inactive during the winter

honeydew—a sugary liquid produced by aphids and scale insects.

host—a living plant or animal that a pest or parasite lives or feeds on.

ichneumon (ik-NEW-mon)—a kind of wasp.

insectary—a place that raises insects for sale or research.

insecticide—a chemical that kills insects.

larva/larvae—the immature stage of an insect's life cycle. Caterpillars are one kind of larvae. (Larvae is the plural form of larva.)

mammals—one group of animals. Some examples of mammals are bears, cats, dogs, cows, rabbits, monkeys, and humans.

mandibles—insect jaws

ovipositor—a thin tube that wasp eggs pass through as the female is laying them.

parasite—an organism that lives on or in another animal or plant (the host). The parasite depends on the host for food and shelter. Some parasites eventually kill their host.

parasitoid—a parasite that kills its host.

pesticide—a chemical that kills pests.

pollen—the male sex cells of green plants.

predator—an animal that kills and eats other animals.

pupa/pupae—the second stage of an insect's life cycle. The larva develops into a pupa. In many cases, the pupa is housed within a cocoon. (Pupae is the plural form of pupa.)

species—a group of organisms that produce viable offspring when they mate.

For Further Reading

Facklam, Howard, and Margery Facklam. *Insects.* New York: Twenty-First Century Books, 1994.

Greenbacker, Liz. *Bugs: Stingers, Suckers, Sweeties, Swingers.* Danbury, Connecticut: Franklin Watts, 1993.

Lee, Sally. *Pesticides.* Danbury, Connecticut: Franklin Watts, 1991.

Perry, Phyllis J. *The Fiddlehoppers: Crickets, Katydids, and Locusts.* Danbury, Connecticut: Franklin Watts, 1995.

Simon, Hilda. *Our Six-Legged Friends and Allies: Ecology in Your Backyard.* New York: Vanguard Press, 1971.

Stokes, Donald W. *A Guide to Observing Insect Lives.* Boston: Little, Brown, 1983.

Zim, Herbert S., and Clarence Cottam. *Insects—A Guide to Familiar American Insects.* Racine, Wisconsin: Western Publishing Co., 1987.

INDEX

ABOUT THE AUTHOR

A former teacher, Sara van Dyck holds a degree in science from the University of Rochester and a master's degree in education. She enjoys observing nature, including stars, plants, birds, tidepool life, and insects. She has written articles on the environment and local history for young people and adults. Ms. van Dyck and her husband live in Santa Monica, California, and have two grandchildren.